SOLVE IT WITH SCIENCE!

THE WATER CYCLE

BY ELIZA NODES

KidHaven PUBLISHING

Published in 2026 by
KidHaven Publishing, an Imprint of Greenhaven Publishing, LLC
2544 Clinton St., Buffalo, NY 14224

Written by: Eliza Nodes
Edited by: Noah Leatherland
Designed by: Rob Delph

Cataloging-in-Publication Data
Names: Nodes, Eliza.
Title: The water cycle / Eliza Nodes.
Description: Buffalo, NY : KidHaven Publishing, 2026. | Series: Solve it with science! | Includes glossary and index.
Identifiers: ISBN 9781534551947 (pbk.) | ISBN 9781534551954 (library bound) | ISBN 9781534551961 (ebook)
Subjects: LCSH: Hydrologic cycle--Juvenile literature.
Classification: LCC GB848.N634 2026 | DDC 551.48--dc23

Printed in China

CPSIA compliance information: Batch #QW26KH: For further information contact Greenhaven Publishing LLC at 1-844-317-7404.

Photo Credits – Images courtesy of Shutterstock.com, unless otherwise stated.

Cover & Recurring – Charcompix, stockphoto-graf, MartiBstock, NartGraphic. 2–3 – Don Pablo, sanbeliaev. 4–5 – Daemyong Prince, PHOTO JUNCTION, AVNik, MelaniWright, Sean-ONeill, Egon Zitter. 6–7 – Natalja Petuhova, Masonjar, Shairaa. 8–9 – Don Pablo, sanbeliaev. 10–11 – POks, Dario Lo Presti. 12–13 – Pokoman, christianthiel.net. 14–15 – Meister Photos, Al Bittler. 16–17 – SCOTTCHAN, Anna Light. 18–19 – Blueastro, IVY PHOTOS. 20–21 – Piyaset, Bilanol, Bernhard Staehli. 22–23 – StockBURIN, Karynf.

CONTENTS

Words that look like this can be found in the glossary on page 24.

WHAT IS THE WATER CYCLE?

The water cycle is the journey water makes around the world. Water can be found on the land, in the sky, in plants, and under the ground. Earth's water is always moving between these places.

Water moves through the water cycle in different ways and in different forms. The water cycle is important to many living things. Plants and animals, including humans, rely on the water cycle to live.

BODIES OF WATER

Most of Earth is covered by water. Areas that are covered by water are called bodies of water. Oceans are the largest bodies of water. Most of Earth's water is stored in oceans.

DID YOU KNOW?

Glaciers contain lots of water stored as ice.

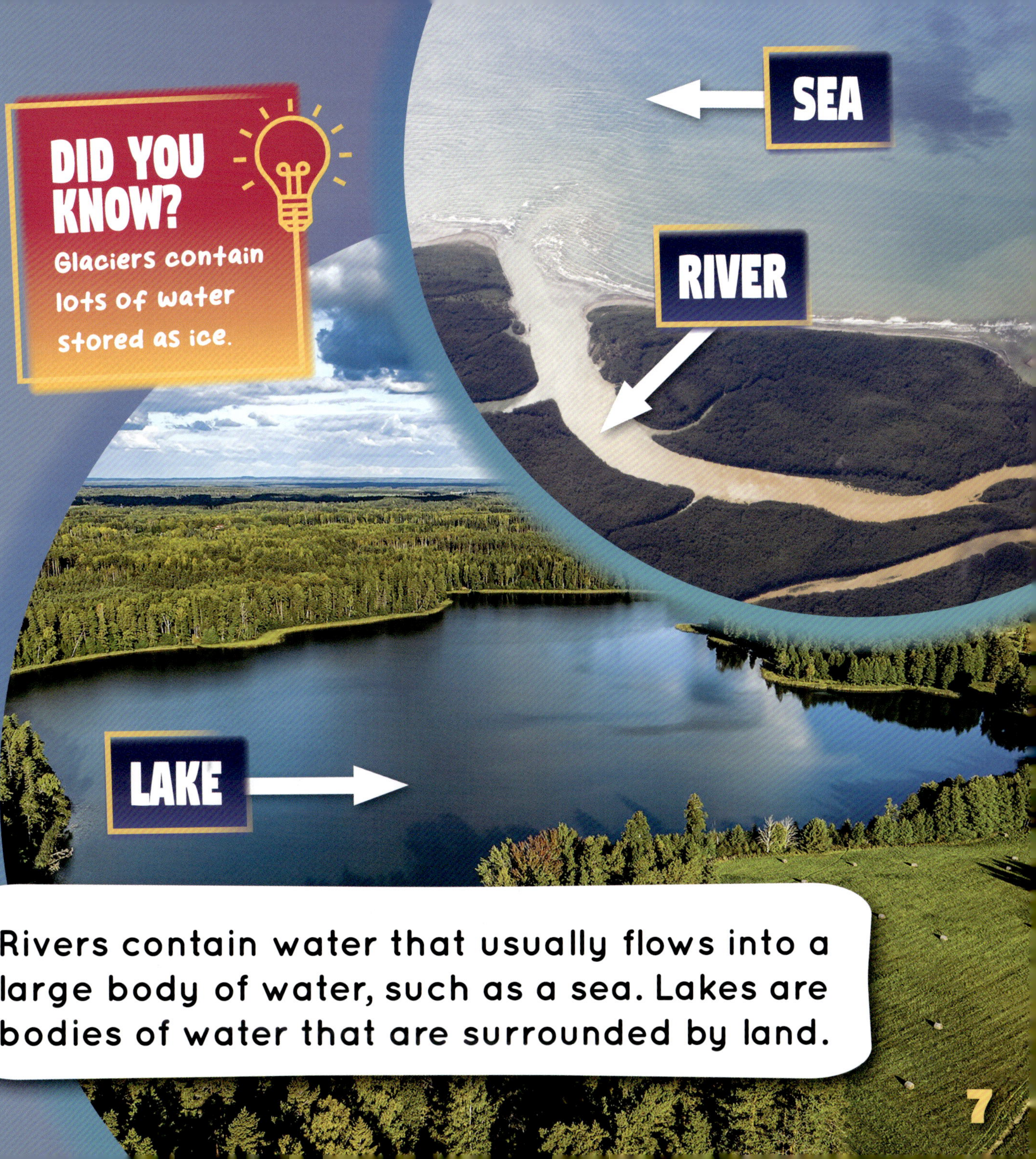

Rivers contain water that usually flows into a large body of water, such as a sea. Lakes are bodies of water that are surrounded by land.

EVAPORATION

Evaporation is one way that water moves through the water cycle. Evaporation happens when a liquid warms up and turns into a gas. The sun heats up water in oceans, seas, rivers, and lakes.

In the water cycle, evaporation moves water into the sky. When water evaporates, it becomes a gas called water vapor. Water vapor moves into the atmosphere.

CONDENSATION

Condensation is when a gas cools down and turns into a liquid. Water vapor cools down high up in Earth's atmosphere. This causes water vapor to condense into water droplets.

These water droplets in the atmosphere are very small. Eventually, they join together to make clouds. Air currents move clouds around the sky. Have you ever watched a cloud move across the sky?

PRECIPITATION

Precipitation is the water that falls from the sky. The water droplets get heavier as they join to form clouds. Eventually, they get too heavy to stay in the air and fall to the ground as rain.

Sometimes, the air is so cold that the water droplets freeze. This turns the water droplets into snow or hail. Snow and hail are also types of precipitation.

RUNOFF AND COLLECTION

Rain and snow fall to the ground. Snow settles on the ground and melts back into water. Water from rain and snow flows over the land. This is called runoff.

Most of this water flows into bodies of water. On land, this is usually rivers and lakes. Sometimes, rain and snow fall straight into bodies of water. This is called collection.

PLANTS

When precipitation falls, some of it soaks into the soil. As it moves through the soil, it collects nutrients.

Plants absorb water from the ground to help them grow. When they absorb the water, they absorb the nutrients.

Plants lose water as part of the water cycle. Water evaporates from their leaves. This is called transpiration.

THE WATER CYCLE

All of Earth's water is connected by the water cycle. Water evaporates and condenses into clouds. It falls as precipitation, known as rain or snow. It is collected back into bodies of water.

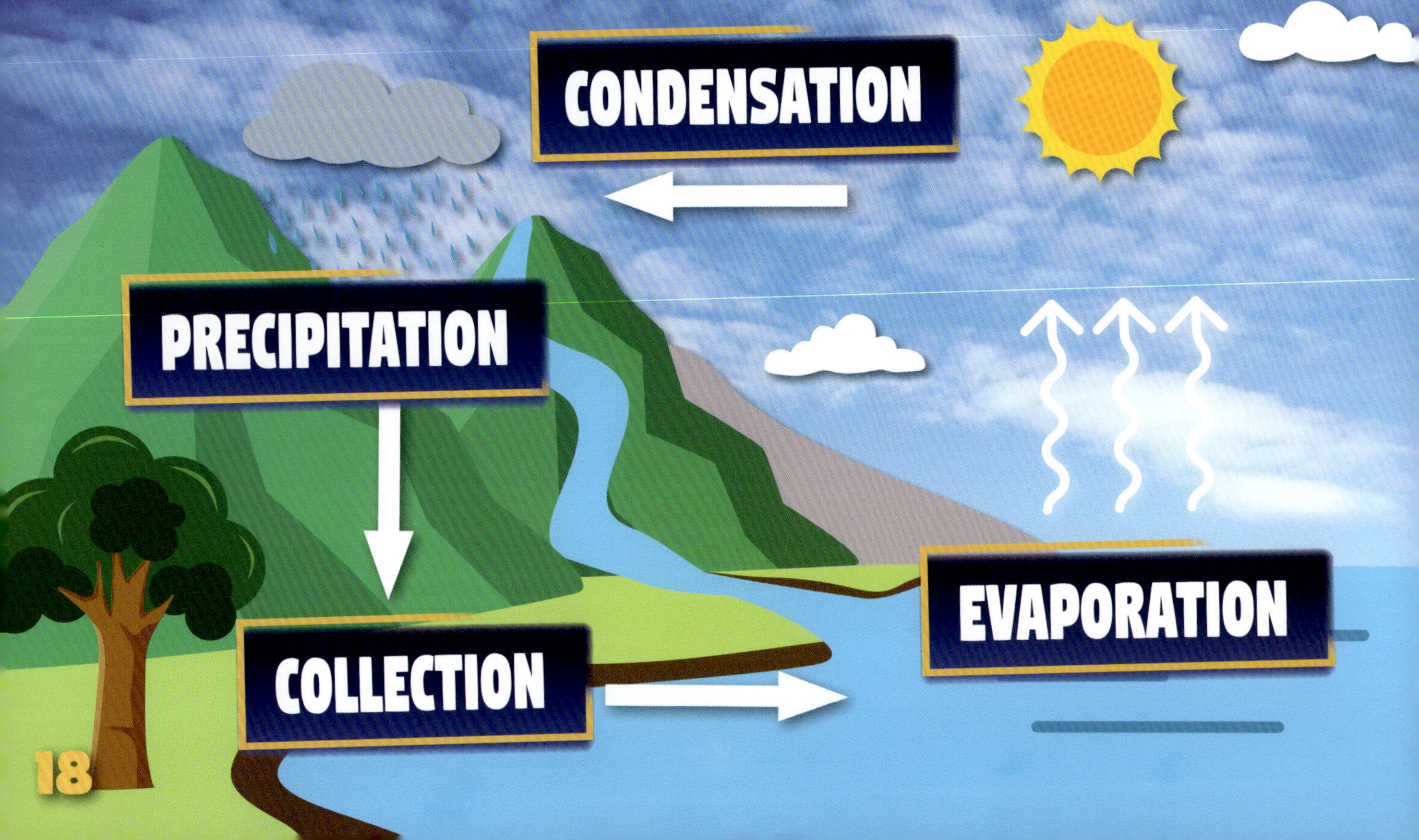

Water is always moving through the water cycle. It happens all over the world. Water might evaporate in one place and fall as rain thousands of miles away.

CLIMATE CHANGE

Climate change is a long-term change to Earth's weather. Climate change is affecting the water cycle.

A FIELD DURING A DROUGHT

Hotter weather means more water is evaporating. This can dry out the ground.

Climate change is causing glaciers to melt. This is making sea levels rise, which is affecting wildlife.

Climate change can affect precipitation. Heavy rainfall in a small area can cause flooding.

ACTIVITIES

Here are some activities to explore the water cycle.

THINK ABOUT IT

Match up the stages of the water cycle listed below with the letters on the diagram.

Answers: A. Evaporation, B. Condensation, C. Precipitation, D. Collection

DO AN EXPERIMENT

Place a cup in a large bowl. Add some water to the bowl. Cover the bowl with plastic wrap and put it outside. See if you can spot the stages of the water cycle happening.

GLOSSARY

ABSORB to take in or soak up

ATMOSPHERE the mixture of gases that make up the air and surround Earth

CURRENTS the movements or flow of things in one direction

DROUGHT a long time without rainfall, which leads to a lack of water

FREEZE when a liquid becomes a solid

GAS a thing that is like air, which spreads out to fill any space available

MELTS when a solid turns into a liquid

NUTRIENTS natural substances that plants and animals need to grow and stay healthy

STORED kept in a certain place

INDEX